W9-CTN-723

This book belongs to:

_____

hide & Seek in hawai'i

A picture game for keiki

Copyright © 1999 by Jane Hopkins

No part of this book may be reproduced in any form or by any electronic
or mechanical means, including information storage and retrieval devices or systems,
without prior written permission from the publisher, except that brief
passages may be quoted for reviews.

All rights reserved

Library of Congress Catalog Card
Number: 99-65464

First Printing, October 1999
Second Printing, April 2000
Third Printing, July 2000
Fourth Printing, November 2000
Fifth Printing, June 2001
Sixth Printing, April 2002
Seventh Printing, January 2003
Eighth Printing, March 2004
Ninth Printing, December 2004
Tenth Printing, October 2005

Design by Jane Hopkins

ISBN 1-56647-278-4

Mutual Publishing, LCC
1215 Center Street, Suite 210
Honolulu, Hawaii 96816
Ph: (808) 732-1709
Fax: (808) 734-4094
e-mail: mutual@mutualpublishing.com
www.mutualpublishing.com

Printed in Korea

hide & Seek in hawai'i

A picture game for keiki

Text and Art Direction by
Jane Hopkins & Ian Gillespie

Photography by

Ray Wong

Mahalo Nui Loa to...

Steven Kop and Sharyl Kapiolani Leleo • Aloha Hula Supply

Jane Yamane • Alaka'i Floral Creations

Bessie Watson • Bessie's Lei Stand

Dorothy Garliepp and Cheryl Moriguchi • The Hunter

Gary Skinner • Kahala Suns

John, Poakalani & Cissy Serrao • Poakalani Hawaiian Quilt Designs

Wayne & Jean Fukuda • Something Special

Glen F. Tomlinson • Koa Surf Classics & The Tomlinson Corporation

Gordon Kai • Ulu Pono Designs

Trent & Trinity Agbayani • Kamiko Akioka • Joy Au • Nelson Char •
Gabrielle Chock • Lynn Cook • Kim Evans • Cara Fradelos • Sarah Frederick •
Leo Gonzalez • David Gulko • Evelyn Hee • David Hershinow • Yuki Kumura • Jeff Lee •
Julie Matsuo • Quinton Kumukahi Matsuo-Chun • Sharon McClure • Ernest & Tasha Miller •
Trevor & Tyson Nakasone • Hugh, Norma & Ian O'Reilly • Edison Sakata • Noe Texeira •
Baron Tomlinson• Ashley Wong • Gay Wong • Kolohe, Bear & Dylan

It's a picture game
of Hide and Seek!

Hawai'i is full of fun things to seek,
lots hide inside, just take a peek…

Hawai'i is a place full of surprises,
where lots of things hide in many disguises.

Look in your hale and outside in the sun
and learn about Hawai'i—it can be fun!

Throughout these pages, I dare you to find
all the things listed within the rhymes.

And when you are done, there's more to read—
learn the Hawaiian word for crab and seed,
and look at the photos all over again,
you will find more from fish to fan!

Table of Contents

May Day is Lei Day
A lei can be worn every day of the week
so many hide what you need to seek...

A bride, a groom and two wedding rings,
and one pair of scissors, among other things.

The letters that spell ALOHA, that's true,
a rocking horse for riding and birthday candle, too.

One long lei needle and one spool of thread,
a crayon and cap for the graduate's head.

Finders Keepers;
Lose Your Slippers

Before going in, take slippers off your feet
then join the party, but first you can seek...

A baseball, four geckos and a happy face,
one plastic flower and a shoe with a lace.

A thumbtack stuck in the bottom of a slipper,
a tic-tac-toe game and someone's black checker.

A golf tee, a penny and a crushed can of soda,
one fishing reel and a paper pagoda.

Surf Da Beach

**Everyday in Hawai'i is a day at the beach,
where I can hide and you can seek.**

Chopsticks left over from lunch by the sea,
two honu, one starfish and someone's lost key.

A message in a bottle and shiny fish hook,
a red rubber band, three butterflies and a book.

A feather, five slippers and a fish made of stone,
two geckos, a whistle and wishing wish bone.

14

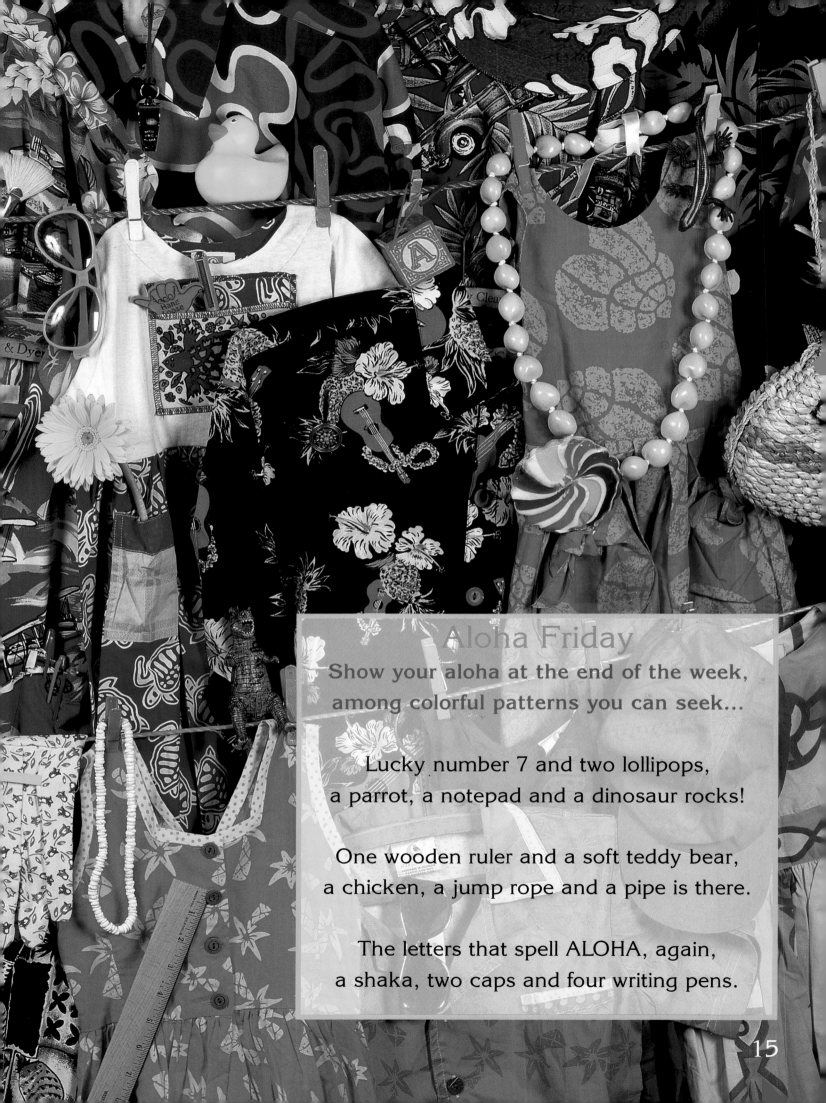

Aloha Friday

Show your aloha at the end of the week,
among colorful patterns you can seek...

Lucky number 7 and two lollipops,
a parrot, a notepad and a dinosaur rocks!

One wooden ruler and a soft teddy bear,
a chicken, a jump rope and a pipe is there.

The letters that spell ALOHA, again,
a shaka, two caps and four writing pens.

Tutu's House

Visiting tutu's house gives you a peek,
where lots of things hide for you to seek...

The word "Honolulu" written three times,
and 59 cents, but not any dimes.

A fan, two ukuleles and one skeleton key,
five spools of thread and the word "History."

One red crayon and a red piece of candy,
the word "OK," and one uneaten "BROWNIE."

17

Wish for Fish

Fishing in Hawai'i cannot be beat,
treasures of the ocean you can always seek...

One lobster, a crab and three fishing reels,
a jellyfish, two honu, but not any eels.

A bottlecap is hiding and three cowry shells,
one spotted pufferfish and two copper bells.

Someone's lost button, is that what I saw?
And the humuhumu-nukunuku-a-pua'a.

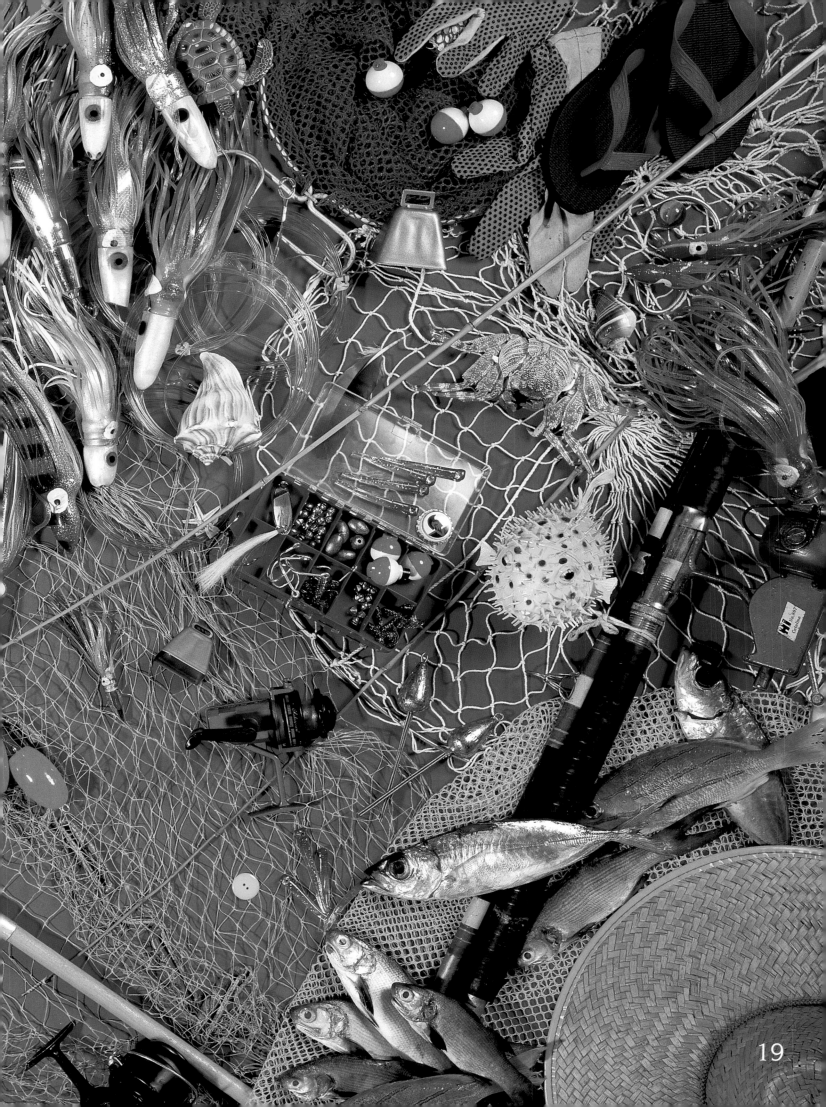

Busy Quilting Bees

The art of quilt-making in Hawai'i runs deep,
because inside the patterns, stories hide and seek...

A cowry shell, a butterfly and four quilting hoops,
four honu, two scissors, and buttons on a loop.

The number 10 and the capital letter Q,
a spool without thread and a shiny ipu.

Another sea shell and a red drawing pencil,
two bird-of-paradise and a quilt-pattern stencil.

21

Dig that Garden

Plants in Hawai'i grow tall and green,
in gardens all over where you can seek...

A birdhouse and glasses for wearing outside,
two golf tees and ribbon for winning 2nd prize.

A tiny red apple, a horse and a bird,
and somewhere a turtle, at least, that's what I've heard.

The letters that spell KALO and a coconut, too,
a rubber duck, a teapot, and a heart just for you.

Hooray for Hula!

To dance the hula is a special treat,
because legends are told for you to seek...

Four pū'ili—split bamboo sticks,
and the letters that spell HULA, just for kicks.

Four cowry shells and two musical ipu,
The "Hawaiian Waltz" and a word that is "Beautiful."

The "Hawaiian Wedding Song" and a carved fish hook,
Two spools of thread and a hair pin, for looks.

25

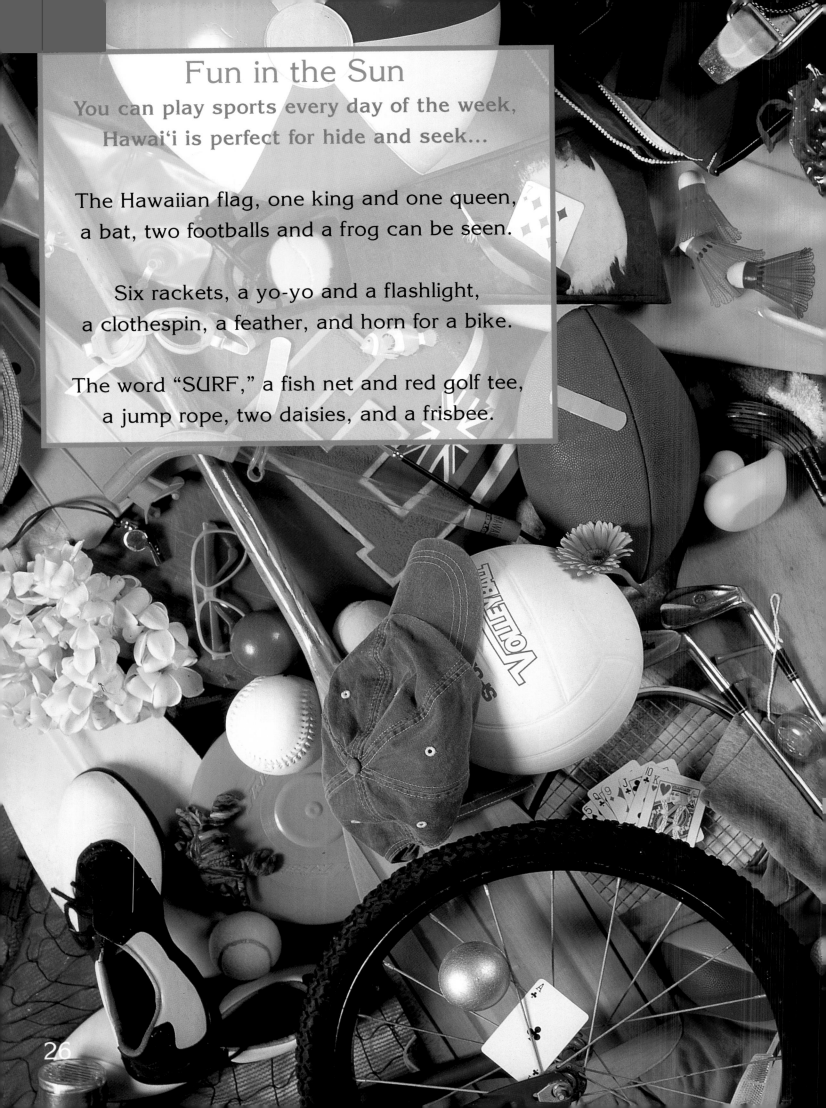

Fun in the Sun

You can play sports every day of the week,
Hawai'i is perfect for hide and seek...

The Hawaiian flag, one king and one queen,
a bat, two footballs and a frog can be seen.

Six rackets, a yo-yo and a flashlight,
a clothespin, a feather, and horn for a bike.

The word "SURF," a fish net and red golf tee,
a jump rope, two daisies, and a frisbee.

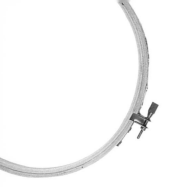

Now look again throughout this book,
go on and try, just take a look.

Learn the Hawaiian word for things,
turn to a page, see what it brings.

When you look again, you just might find
something new you left behind.

Share your aloha every day of the week,
keep your eyes open and play hide and seek!

28

All these things hide for you to seek...

English	Hawaiian
apple	ʻāpala
banana	maiʻa
baseball	kinipōpō
baseball bat	lāʻau kinipōpō
beach chair	noho ʻopiʻopi
bell	pele
bicycle	paikikala
bird	manu
birdhouse	hale manu
book	puke
bottle	ʻōmole
bowl	ʻumeke
bracelet	kūpeʻe
brush	palaki lauoho
bucket	pākeke
butterfly	pulelehua
button	pihi
camera	pahupaʻikiʻi
candle	ihoiho
candy	kanakē
chopsticks	lāʻauʻai

29

English	Hawaiian
cigar	kīkā
clock	uaki
clothesline	kaula kaula'i lole
clothespin	pine kaula'i
coconut	niu
coins	kālā pa'a
conch shell	pū'olē'olē
cork	'umoki
cowry shell	leho
crab	pāpa'i
doll	ki'i
dollar	kālā
drum	pahu
duck	kakā
eye glasses	makaaniani
fan	pe'ahi
feather	hulu
fish	i'a
fishing pole	mākoi
fish hook	makau
flag	hae
football	kinipōpō peku
frog	poloka
garden	māla
gecko	mo'o
gloves	mīkini lima
guava	kuawa
handkerchief	hainakā pa'eke

English	Hawaiian
hat	pāpale
helmet	mahiole
horse	lio lāʻau
hose	ʻiliwai
jacks	kimo
jar	poho aniani
jewelry	lako kula
key	kī
lantern	ipukukui hele pō
marble	kinikini
mirror	aniani
music	pila hoʻokani
necklace	lei
lei needle	mākila
net	ʻupena
newspaper	nūpepa
papaya	mīkana
penny	keneka
perfume	lūkini
photograph	kiʻi
pick axe	kipikua
pin cushion	pulu kui
pin	kui
pineapple	hala kahiki
pipe	ipu paka
plant	lāʻau
pot	poho mea kanu
purse	ʻekeʻeke

English	Hawaiian
rainbow	ānuenue
rake	kope
ribbon	lipine
ring	komo kula
rocks	pōhaku
rope	kaula
safety pin	pine kaiapa
scissors	ʻūpā
seeds	ʻanoʻano
sewing machine	mīkini humuhumu
shirt	palaka aloha
shoe	kāmaʻa
shovel	kopalā
slipper	kāmaʻa pale wāwae
spool of thread	pōkaʻa lopi
spoon	puna nui
starfish	peʻa
string	kaula
surfboard	papa heʻe nalu
tennis racket	lāʻau paʻi kinipōpō
towel	kāwele
train	kaʻaahi
turtle	honu
umbrella	hoʻomāmalu

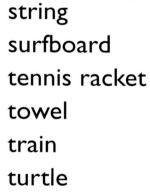